AF615349

J
920
MAR

CONTEMPORARY AMERICAN SUCCESS STORIES

Famous People of Asian Ancestry

Volume I

Barbara J. Marvis

A Mitchell Lane
Multicultural Biography Series

CONTEMPORARY AMERICAN SUCCESS STORIES
Famous People of Asian Ancestry

VOLUME I
Pat Suzuki
Minoru Yamasaki
Kristi Yamaguchi
An Wang
Connie Chung
Carlos Bulosan

VOLUME II
Dalip Singh Saund
Patsy Takemoto Mink
Daniel Ken Inouye
Yoshiko Uchida
Haing Ngor

VOLUME III
Samuel Hayakawa
Vivian Kim
Isamu Noguchi
Ida Chen
Michael Chang

Design and composition: SJS Associates

Library of Congress Catalog Card Number: 93-78991

Printed and bound in the United States of America

ISBN 1-883845-00-9 hardcover
ISBN 1-883845-06-8 softcover

TABLE OF CONTENTS

Acknowledgements

All reasonable effort has been made to obtain copyright permission where such permission has been deemed necessary. Any oversight brought to the publisher's attention will be corrected in future printings. Quotations reprinted from *Lessons*, An Wang,©1986 by Wang Institute of Graduate Studies, reprinted by permission of Addison-Wesley Publishing Co., Redding, MA.

We wish to acknowledge with gratitude the generous cooperation of Pat Suzuki and her sister, June Mochizuki in the compilation of the story about and photographs of Pat Suzuki; Mrs. Teruko Yamasaki, Cynthia Waderlow, and Taro Yamasaki for information and photographs about Minoru Yamasaki; and Carole Yamaguchi for information and photographs about her daughter Kristi. Grateful acknowledgement is also made to Martin Silverstein from CBS/Media Relations. Special thanks to Florence Hongo of the Japanese American Curriculum Project in San Mateo, California for helping with our selection and location of the people profiled in this series.

Photo Credits

Cover photo, Barbara Marvis, p.8, p.16 courtesy Pat Suzuki; p.11, p.12, p.17, p.18, p.20 courtesy June Mochizuki; p.22, p.26, p.33, p.39 courtesy Teruko Yamasaki; p.37 Barbara Marvis; p.42, p.47, p.49, p.53 courtesy Carole Yamaguchi; p.51 Bettman; p.54, p.63 AP/Wide World Photos; p.64, p.77 courtesy CBS; p.70 AP/Wide World Photos; p.75 Bettman; p.78, p.84, p.87 Special Collections Division, University of Washington Libraries, negative nos. WW2710, WW512, WW513.

PREFACE

More people live in Asia than on any other continent. The continent of Asia is located east of Europe. Asia is so large that the northern border touches the Arctic circle. It is divided by an imaginary line that runs from the Ural Mountains, to the Caspian Sea, and then through the Black Sea.

The people of Asia are divided into two races: Asian and Indian. The Asians include most of the people of China, Japan, Korea, Taiwan, Vietnam, Laos, Cambodia, the Philippines, and most of the other people in southeast Asia. The other major race is Indian. Most of the Indians came from India and the surrounding areas.

People all over the world have the same needs, but they meet these needs in different ways. They learned their way of thinking and acting from their ancestors. These traditions are called culture. People living in Asia have a distinct culture as do people living in many other parts of the world. People who came to America from Asia or other places may carry some of this culture to their new homeland. Then they learn new ways of doing things from other people in America. Some of their original traditions may change. Pretty soon, these immigrants are no longer Asians, but they are Americans. We sometimes refer to people by their ancestry, since most people are proud of their heritage. So this book refers to Asian Americans as people whose ancestors came from Asia. But, they are really all Americans, because everyone in the United States, except the Native Americans, has ancestors who originally came from somewhere else in the world. Even a first generation immigrant who makes his life in the United States, is an American.

Sometimes it is difficult to look at a person and tell where his or her ancestors might have come from. But certain people have distinctive looks that allow us to easily distinguish them from others. One of the problems that Americans of Asian ancestry have faced is that they are easily distinguished by their looks. The Asian Americans are often subjected to racism and ethnic prejudice as are other distinguishable groups of Americans. The Asians who came to America had many different customs and beliefs compared to people of other immigration groups. Not many Americans understood their way of life. So they have been met with prejudice and distrust over the years.

For many years, Asians were not permitted to come to the United States, or they were permitted in restricted numbers. The Chinese Exclusion Act of 1882 was among the first laws to effectively keep the Chinese and Japanese from emigrating to the U.S. The Immigration Act of 1924 prohibited any people who were not eligible for citizenship from coming to the United States. At that time, only Caucasians and black people of African descent were eligible for citizenship. The reason for the Exclusion Act was to preserve jobs for American workers that had been going to Asian immigrants.

During World War II, the Japanese Americans faced additional problems after Japan bombed Pearl Harbor, Hawaii. Some people said that the Japanese Americans in Hawaii helped Japan with the bombing. But, this is not so. The Japanese Americans contributed greatly to the war effort for America. Nevertheless, on February 19, 1942 President Franklin D. Roosevelt signed executive order number 9066, which relocated more than 110,000 Japanese Americans from the three westernmost states from their homes to centralized camps, generally not fit for human inhabitation. Two-thirds of these people were American citizens born here in the United States. Most of the people in the camps were there only because they were unable to find other places to go before the mass-evacuation order was issued. There were ten relocation areas, managed by the civilian War Relocation Authority, in undeveloped regions of Arizona, California, Utah, Wyoming, Colorado, and Arkansas. Merely because of their race, these Japanese Americans were denied their rights as American citizens. Though the safety of the country was the reason for this relocation, it is not understood why German Americans were not also relocated during this time, since Germany was the main aggressor in World War II.

It was not until 1943 that President Roosevelt allowed nisei (nee-sayee; second-generation Japanese American) young men to volunteer for service in the United States Army. Immediately, ten thousand Japanese American men, eighty-percent of those who were eligible, volunteered to prove their loyalty to *their* land. Many of these young men served in the famed, and much decorated 442nd Regimental Combat Team.

The people of the United States are descendants of a long migration. The roots of our nation reach out to all continents of the globe. We are a people woven of many strands. The mix of culture affects every aspect of our lives. Someday, we may all learn to live with one another, respecting our differences while treasuring the things we share.

This book chronicles the lives of six great Asian Americans who have made notable contributions to American society.

Commonwealth of Independent States
Ural Mountains
Black Sea
Turkey
Syria
Caspian Sea
Mongolia
North Korea
Japan
South Korea
Iraq
Iran
China
PACIFIC OCEAN
Afghan-istan
Saudi Arabia
Pakistan
(Myanmar)
Taiwan
Burma
Laos
India
ARABIAN SEA
Thai-land
Philippines
Vietnam
BAY OF BENGAL
Cambodia
Malaysia
Indonesia

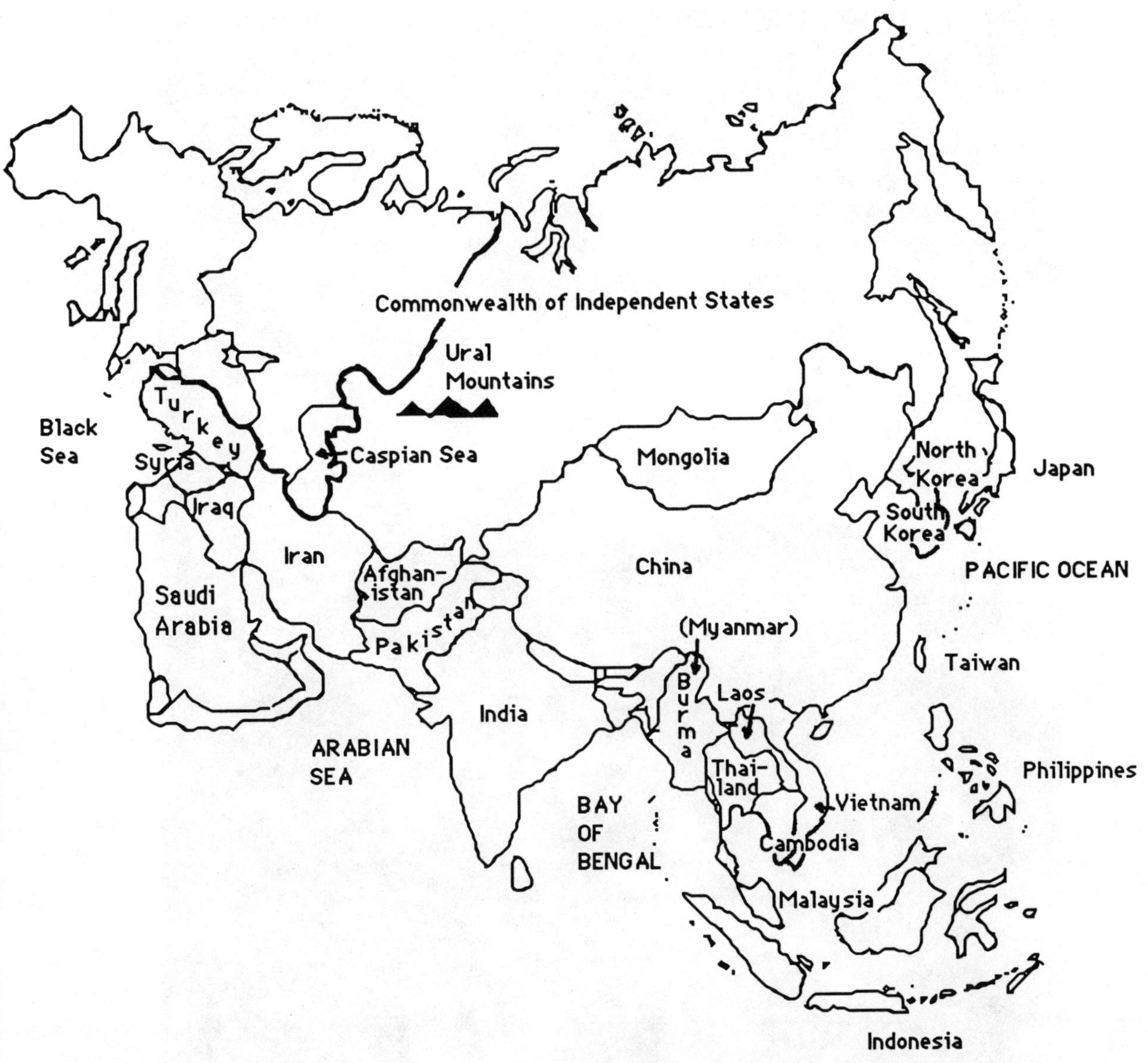

ASIA

PAT SUZUKI

Singer, Actress
1930-

"My Poppa always told me, 'Ya gotta think big, work hard, and have a dream.'"

Pat Suzuki, July 1993

AS YOU READ

- Pat was never very happy growing up on a farm in Cressey, California. Read to find out what she would have rather been doing. Did she realize her dreams?
- Pat really became an actress by accident. Read to find out what she had set out to do when she became a singer and an actress.
- Pat was married and then divorced several years later. But she and her former husband remained close friends. As you read, see if you can determine what it is about Pat's personality that might make it difficult for her to live with one person for a long period of time.

PAT SUZUKI

Pat Suzuki has always been the little girl with the big dreams. Intent on living her life one day at a time, Pat has nevertheless worked hard to realize her dreams of being in show business and seeing the world. What Pat lacks in height (she is only five feet tall) she makes up for in charm and character. Never at a loss for words, Pat once told a newspaper reporter that her aim in life was to make a fortune, see the world, and settle down on a non-working farm. Pat looks back on her life now and says, "I treasure my good friends, reading, painting, and traveling," and now that she is no longer performing, she intends to sit back and really enjoy the flowers.

Pat once told a newspaper reporter that her aim in life was to make a fortune, see the world, and settle down on a non-working farm.

Born on September 23, 1930 in the small California village of Cressey, Chiyoko (Pat) Suzuki was the youngest of four children born to Aki (Okamoto) and Chiyosaku Suzuki. She was named after her father. She has an older brother, Frank, born in 1921; an older sister, Mary, born in 1923; and another older sister, June, born in 1925. Both of her parents were born in Toyohashi, Japan, and immigrated to the United States where they owned and worked a one-hundred acre fruit farm. They grew almonds, grapes, and peaches.

Pat remembers her mother as an exceedingly talented singer and musician who always set high goals and standards for her children to attain.

She gave music instruction for Pat's sisters, but Pat said, "She gave up on me!" Pat remembers that her mother read constantly in her spare time, and it is a safe bet that Pat's love of reading and her singing talent were inherited from her mother. Pat still has memories of her mother's beautiful flower arrangements. Pat's father was a very understanding, loving parent who Pat describes as "wise, mellow, and fair-minded." He always seemed to have time for Pat. Pat says she had a very special relationship with her father. "I adored him," she says. "He took me to films and the fair. We could have great talks about anything. He had a wonderful sense of humor."

Pat's parents, Aki and Chiyosaku Suzuki

As the youngest of the four children, Pat figured she was supposed to take care of herself. Her family called her "Chiby," which means squirt, but she became known as Pat, because the local grocer could not pronounce her given name, Chiyoko. As she was growing up, Pat had the feeling that her brothers and sisters were much, much older than she was. "I could hardly wait to grow up," recalls Pat in a *Time Magazine* interview conducted when she was in her twenties. "I didn't like being a kid because I always had certain feelings I couldn't

Pat during the early days of her acting career.

explain. The only things I could dream about in those days were the trucks going by on the highway all night long. I used to dream of all the places they had been that I would like to go some day." Pat described herself as a loner, who loved nature, music, art, fantasy, and reading. To this day, Pat is still fascinated with truck drivers.

Pat went to elementary school in a two-room schoolhouse in Cressey. She liked to ride horses bareback and she learned to swim in the irrigation canals on her father's farm. She learned to speak Spanish with the Mexican workers who picked peaches for her father. She played "theatre" with her neighborhood friends, stacking grape lug boxes into a stage. One day as she walked home from school, she decided to take a shortcut when she encountered a strange dog that she had not seen before. The dog did not like Pat on his territory and set about to bite her on her hind end! That was a shortcut Pat never took again! Her sister June says Pat was very bright and outgoing and always had a cheery smile. By the time she was in fifth grade, she could read on a tenth grade level; Pat sat up listening to the election returns and tallying results on the night Roosevelt was elected. But nothing in this time of her life seemed like any fun to Pat. There was nowhere to go. Pat wanted to see the world.

One of Pat's joys when she was growing up was that she loved to sing. She taught herself songs from listening to the family phonograph. She sang solos in her church choir and at county fairs. She sang her first solo in Sunday school when she was only five. She had joined in singing with the rest of the class, but soon she could be heard above them all. The rest of the children stopped singing to let Pat go it alone. Her sister June says that Pat got all the singing talent in the family. June remembers that by the time Pat was in sixth grade, she knew all the words to the opera *Carmen* from singing along with the recording. She often sang at weddings and other events accompanied on the piano by her sister Mary.

But singing was not foremost on her mind when the United States entered World War II after the attack on Pearl Harbor. Pat was only eleven years old. During one of her last public performances, she sang *God Bless America* and, according to June, everyone was very moved by her rendition. Shortly thereafter, the entire family was relocated to the Amache, Colorado camp. Pat found she had to continue her schooling in the relocation camp. Like so many other Japanese Americans, Pat's family had to give up most everything they owned. Pat says she remembers the camp—the barbed wire fences and the duststorms. After the war, the family stayed for a year in Colorado and had a sugar-beet farm. In 1946, they returned to their California farm and Pat finished school at Livingston High School in the San Joaquin Valley. But for Pat, things were still as bad as ever. "I absolutely hated high school," says Pat, "I wasn't very popular, but I did persist because it was expected of me to get through and go on to college. A lot of other creative-type people I've known admit feeling that they never fit in at all, either."

"I absolutely hated high school," says Pat, "I wasn't very popular, but I did persist because it was ex-pected of me to get through and go on to college."

Pat's imagination, her reading, and her love of music are what got her through her childhood. She loved to listen to the radio with her brother. She heard music from the Edgewater Beach Hotel and decided she wanted to see Chicago. She could imagine just what the beach and hotel looked like. When she would see a painting, she wanted to go visit the place the artist had painted. Pat couldn't wait to grow up and get out on her own.

In 1948, Pat enrolled at Mills College in Oakland where her sister June was interning. Then she transferred to Modesto Junior College near her home, and later San Francisco City College. Pat says San Francisco City College opened up a whole new world for her—she went to the theatre and to concerts and took ballet classes. She met new friends and discovered a new way of thinking. Her parents were not entirely happy with Pat's new outlook on life, however, and they thought that she should settle down at the more conservative San Jose State College. She paid for her college education by working part-time jobs, including weekend singing stints at a nightclub. She worked as a typist, did odd jobs at school, and worked the phones at a Chinese take-out restaurant.

"I was a big slob," says Pat of her days in college. She did not act like other Japanese Americans and her friends were mostly other Caucasians instead of other nisei (second-generation Japanese American). This caused much criticism from family and friends and resulted in many heartaches for Pat during those days.

Pat graduated from San Jose State in 1954 with a Bachelor of Arts degree. She did post graduate work in education, thinking maybe she would teach someday. Though her sister Mary did teach school in Chicago at Parker, Pat just never got around to it. She set off to begin her dream of touring Europe before she began her teaching career. However, she ran short of money when she got to New York City and she found a job as a walk-on in a road production of *Teahouse of the August Moon* with Burgess Meredith. The production traveled to the west coast. They were playing in Seattle, Washington where Pat sat in on a jam session at the Colony Club. Owner Norm Bobrow offered her a singing job immediately. Under his guidance, Pat developed a local following. Soon, Bing Crosby discovered her and with his praise, her reputation as a singer grew. A great deal of her attraction came from the contrast between her vitality and her stature. The five-foot-tall button-nosed nisei sang with a booming, brassy voice that "...all but rattled the ice in the highballs..." according to *Time* (July 22, 1957).

Pat recording her album for RCA.

In 1957, Pat signed a contract with Vik Records, a subsidiary of RCA. In 1958, Vik Records released an album by Pat called *The Many Sides of Pat Suzuki.* Bing Crosby wrote the jacket notes for the album. It was an instant success. Her first single record for Vik, *Daddy,* became a best seller almost overnight. She went back to New York City for promotional appearances on Jack Parr, where she made a week-long appearance. At the end of the week, Parr asked her to stay on longer, but Pat said, "I'm going home to Seattle... Seattle is my home." But as it turned out, Pat later chose to live in New York City instead of the west coast.

The jacket cover to Pat's first album.

That summer, Pat starred as Dorothy in *The Wizard of Oz* at the Starlite Theatre in Kansas City. Later that year, Pat won the Downbeat National Disc Jockey Poll as "America's best new female singer of 1958."

In June 1958, after another appearance on the Jack Parr show, Pat won a leading role in the famous Rodgers and Hammerstein musical, *The Flower Drum Song*. Pat starred with Miyoshi

PAT SUZUKI

Umeki who played a picture bride from China who comes to the United States to marry a Chinese American in San Francisco's Chinatown. Pat played Linda Low, a Chinese American dancer who chose to live American style instead of by Chinese tradition, and almost takes the groom away from the would-be bride. The critics loved Pat's voice as she belted out such now-famous songs as "I Enjoy Being a Girl." The show opened in Boston on October 27, 1958, began in New York at the St. James Theatre on December 1, 1958, and completed its Broadway run on May 7, 1960. Tickets were in such demand that Pat often had difficulty getting them for her own family. By the time *The Flower Drum Song* closed on Broadway, Pat Suzuki had become a familiar face on TV and in newspaper feature columns.

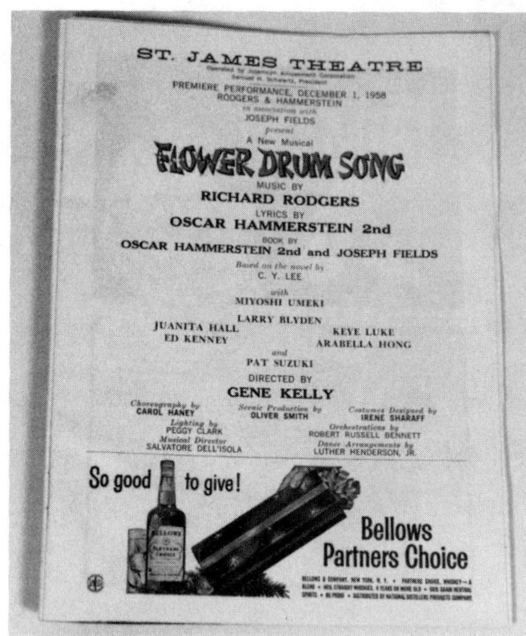

Pat starred in the *Flower Drum Song*, a major Broadway play.

After *The Flower Drum Song* opened, Pat did many more television appearances including an interview on Edward R. Murrow's *Person to Person* show, a program on which most people in public life dreamed of appearing. She was on the Ed Sullivan Show, and she performed on a *Voice of Firestone* program featuring the music of Richard Rodgers on May 4, 1959. She sang at the Newport, Rhode Island Jazz Festival in July 1959.

During her Broadway run, Pat was on location for a huge *Ladies Home Journal* ad campaign when she met her future husband, Mark Shaw. Mr. Shaw was a famous fashion photographer and contributing photographer to *Life Magazine.* He had traveled the world, something that held great fascination for Pat. He and Pat became best friends. On March 28, 1960, she and Mark were married in Baltimore's First Unitarian Church. She made her regular appearance that night in *The Flower Drum Song* and kept her wedding a secret from the other performers.

Pat made many television appearances including an interview on Edward R. Murrow's *Person to Person* Show...

Assignments took Mark around the world and Pat was able to accompany him on many trips. Later in 1960, their son David was born. Pat went on to perform in a production of *Irma La Douce* and then traveled in a national road company tour in the United States and Canada in *The Owl and the Pussycat* with Robert Reed who later starred in *The Brady Bunch*. Though her marriage to Mark Shaw did not last and they were divorced in the late sixties, she and Mark remained close friends until his death in 1969.

Pat Suzuki

Pat continued with her lifelong dream of traveling the world and has made many trips to

Pat (middle) with sisters Mary (right) and June (left).

Europe and Asia, including Japan. She received many music and theatre awards. David is grown now and was married one year ago to Juliet Cuming. Both David and his new wife are filmmakers. Pat's brother Frank is married to Maryon and lives in Cressey, California, where the family was raised. He and his wife have five daughters. Her sister Mary died in the early

1980's. Until then, she lived in Chicago and taught school at the Parker Institute. She was married to Harry Sabusawa, whose sister Mari married James Michener, author of *Tales of the South Pacific* and *Hawaii*, and many other best sellers. She had three daughters and one son. Her sister June is married to Minoru Mochizuki, who was a pastor at Western Michigan University. They raised five children and currently live in Denver, Colorado.

"If you meet Pat Suzuki, be prepared for anything," wrote Sally Hammond in the New York *Post* (May 19, 1958). "She's apt to skip onto the sidewalk and fling her arms toward the sun. Or she'll soberly confide her philosophy of singing...Pat is the farthest cry from the stereotyped Japanese female—that submissive, delicate, kimono-clad creature." Today, Pat Suzuki can be described in much the same manner. Though she may not do as much skipping anymore, her attitude and zest for life are without bounds. Says Pat, "At this point in my life, I intend to enjoy the flowers." This little nisei thought big, worked hard, and saw her dreams come true.

MINORU YAMASAKI

1912-1986
Architect

“Today our technology has brought a chaos. We have speed, traffic, fear, congestion, and restlessness. We need a place to put our lives in balance. Architecture is a good place for this. When people go into good buildings, there should be serenity and delight.

“Most of the great architecture of the past was built for monumental purposes—to impress or awe the masses. Our democratic ideals need buildings that give us instead a sense of awe, a sense of happiness, peace, security.”

"Serenity and Delight," *Time Magazine*, September 14, 1959

AS YOU READ

- Minoru Yamasaki dedicated his life to designing buildings that he thought would bring pleasure to others. Yet he was highly criticized by other architects for much of his work. In his lifetime, he did not hear the overwhelming praise that his architecture has brought since his death. Why do you think he knew mostly about the criticism instead of the praise?

- Yamasaki was dedicated to having his buildings built "his" way. In fact, during disagreements with engineers and clients, he would often walk away from a project and say, "I quit," if he felt a change would compromise the quality of his building. During the design and building of the World Trade Center, Yamasaki held out for his structural design. In 1993, terrorists tried to blow up the World Trade Center, but it did not fall down. What do you think this says for Yamasaki's determination?

Minoru Yamasaki

For Minoru Yamasaki, architecture was not a way of life, it was his life. No matter where he was or what he was doing, he constantly thought about the problems involved in the buildings he was working on. Many times, he would see his work in his dreams. One day he got out of bed at 3 am in the morning to sketch a totally new concept for a set of buildings that he had just dreamt about. Later, that complex became the Century Plaza Towers in Los Angeles, California, and it was built almost exactly as Yamasaki had dreamed it. "It is experiences such as this one," Yamasaki wrote, "where, quite literally, my dream does come true, that give me personal fulfillment in my career."

Often at the center of controversy, the five-foot-five Minoru Yamasaki never looked like a man to brew up such a storm. Most famous for his design of the Twin Towers for the World Trade Center on Manhattan's Lower West Side, the Detroit headquarters of Reynolds Metal Co., and the Lambert-St. Louis Municipal Airport, Yamasaki was a talented architect, a small, slight man, with a gently explosive sense of humor. Accused of breaking architectural rules and outraging the architectural know-it-alls, Yamasaki designed his buildings with pools of water, plants, skylights and courts, domes and vaults, arches and colonades, elaborate designs intended to enhance the lives of those people who enter or see them.

Minoru (meaning "bearing fruit") Yamasaki (meaning "mountain ledge with a great view") was born on December 1, 1912, in Seattle, Washington to John Tsunejiro Yamasaki and Hana (Ito) Yamasaki, who had recently emigrated to the United States. His father was a salesman and his mother was a homemaker. He had a brother, Ken, who became a physician.

Yamasaki designed his buildings with pools of water, plants, skylights and courts, domes and vaults, arches and colonades...

His father was the third son of a Japanese farmer, who owned a large rice farm in Toyama, on the western shore of the main island of Honshu. His family lived in a very comfortable house. Traditionally, in Japan, the eldest son inherits the entire estate in order to keep the family lands intact. This was the case in John's family, and it meant that John was destined to stay and work on the farm all his life. But John wanted a future beyond the farm, and he came to Seattle in 1908 to join his second brother when the farm in Japan was inherited by the oldest son.

His mother, Hana, was the oldest child in a family of twelve. When her mother and father moved to America with several of the older children, Hana was left behind to care for the younger ones. After some years, the family was reunited in Seattle, where her father had established a business as a tailor.

His mother and father were introduced to each other through a go-between, which is the custom in Japan. They were married and set about to raise their family in Seattle. But both his mother and father had gone to high school in Japan, and the language and the customs were very foreign to them here in the United States. There was also strong racial prejudice on the west coast at that time against Asian Americans, and Minoru understood years later, that his parents were ill-prepared to help him grow up and prepare for his own future in America.

Minoru's parents, Hana and John Yamasaki

The first years of Minoru's life were spent in a shabby, run-down tenement that was perched on a hill in the Yesler Hill section of Seattle. Yamasaki said the foundation had eroded so badly that the house tilted to one side. He felt that at any moment, the house might slide down the slope to the street below! There was an outhouse at the rear of the building and only cold running water indoors. But Minoru remembers his first home as a place that was fun to live. He and his friends used to play in a cave nearby where they would hide their most precious belongings.

Minoru started public school while his family still lived in the tenement. His mother made him dress up every day with a large bow tie and dress pants. This prompted the neighborhood children to call him "Sissy," which made Minoru feel very bad. He constantly begged his mother to let him dress like the other boys, but she insisted he be "properly dressed." One day after school, the baseball team was short of players and Minoru was placed in the outfield. He accidently caught what was certain to have been a home run, and he was immediately accepted by his peers. Minoru insisted that evening at home that he no longer be dressed as a "Sissy," and after a long argument, he finally won.

After a few years, the family was able to move into a flat with an indoor bathroom and both hot and cold running water. His father had to work very hard to afford these accommodations for his family and he often worked two or three jobs at a time. Minoru remembers helping his father clean the floors of a chocolate factory on Sunday mornings. Mostly he remembers the

The first years of Minoru's life were spent in a shabby, run-down tenement that was perched on a hill in the Yesler Hill section of Seattle.

smell of all that good chocolate, and he was never allowed to have a single piece.

During those years, Minoru was sheltered from much of the anti-Japanese discrimination he later experienced because the Japanese community stayed pretty much to itself. But even so, Yamasaki experienced enough racial bias during this time. He did not become involved in any crusades to resolve the problems brought about by this prejudice, but devoted himself to his studies, instead. Yamasaki remembers one incident, however, where his mother came home in tears after a cruel experience on a bus. She had taken a seat next to a white woman, who rose and changed seats to get away from "the Japanese woman." "A word that I heard over and over again whenever there would be an incident or a slight was *shikataganai*, which means, 'it can't be helped.'" This attitude was very prevalent in the Japanese community in the early part of the twentieth century.

"I am bewildered that a color difference can create prejudice," Yamasaki wrote in *A Life in Architecture* (Weatherhill). "I am a firm believer that all people, whatever their color, race, or creed, should be recognized for their character and for their contributions to society...The human race would gain tremendously if we would cleanse ourselves of discrimination in all areas.

If all human beings were given the opportunity to achieve their highest degree of capability without suppression, our world would be a much better place."

Yamasaki attended Garfield High School in Seattle. He was most interested in math and the sciences and he did very well in these areas. He followed the usual high school routine, but he was not particularly excited about any one field of study. Then, in 1926, when he was a sophomore, his uncle, his mother's brother Koken Ito, came to stay for awhile at the Yamasaki home. Ito had earned an architectural degree at the University of California at Berkeley. After graduation, he had been promised a job in Chicago and he stopped to visit the Yamasaki family on his way there. He was working on some drawings in his room when he noticed that Minoru was fascinated by what he was doing. "The more my uncle talked about architecture, the more I wanted to become an architect," Yamasaki said. Ito later returned to Tokyo to practice his profession because foreign-born Asians could not become U.S. citizens at that time, and therefore, he could not become a licensed architect. He went on to work for the Ohbayashi Company, one of the largest construction companies in Japan. Because he was bilingual, he was often sent back to the United States on various projects, and Minoru saw him occasionally throughout the years.

"I am bewildered that a color difference can create prejudice. I am a firm believer that all people, whatever their color, race, or creed, should be recognized for their character..."

MINORU YAMASAKI

Yamasaki graduated from Garfield High in 1929. He wanted to go to college, but his family had no money to send him. He had to earn nearly all of it himself. He spent five summers doing grueling work in Alaskan fish canneries for $50 a month. During the busy periods, he worked from 4 am in the morning until midnight. His meals were salmon and rice for lunch and rice and salmon for dinner; the accommodations were very poor: once he was housed in one room with one hundred men in bunks with bedbugs. The men were up all night with flashlights trying to kill the bugs. However, the $200 he earned each summer helped pay his way through the University of Washington.

In college, Yamasaki was often torn between majoring in architecture or engineering. Since he was good in math and science, he often thought he would make a good engineer. He was quite unprepared for the art, sculpture, and watercolor classes he had to take in preparation for his career in architecture. But he found that with some hard work and determination, he did very well in his classes, and he was eager to move ahead into the world of active architecture.

He earned his Bachelor of Architecture degree in 1934, but it was the middle of the Depression and there was so much anti-Japanese discrimination around Seattle at that time, Yamasaki decided to go to New York to pursue his architectural career. He arrived in Manhattan in September 1934 with $40 to his name.

Yamasaki quickly learned that this was no time to begin his career. He found no architectural jobs available. He spent his first year in Manhattan wrapping china for Morimura Brothers, the Japanese importing firm that distributed Noritake china. In 1935, during a week's vacation, he volunteered his services to the New York architectural firm of Githens and Keally. He was given his first professional job as a designer for the firm, and he worked for them from 1935 to 1937. In the meantime, he was doing graduate work and teaching water color at New York University. In 1937, Yamasaki joined the firm of Shreve, Lamb & Harmon, who had designed the Empire State Building.

In 1941, he met and fell in love with Teruko Hirashiki, who had come to New York from Los Angeles to study piano at the Juliard School of Music. They were married on December 5, 1941, three months after they had met and two days before the bombing of Pearl Harbor. A co-worker insisted on drilling Yamasaki about the war and decided that Minoru must have known about the attack on Pearl Harbor since he planned his marriage just two days before it was to take place!

In college, Yamasaki was often torn between majoring in architecture or engineering.

Yamasaki did not lose his job after the bombing of Pearl Harbor as many other Japanese Americans did. "You are one of our best men," said Richmond Shreve, "and I'm going to back you all the way." But, back in Seattle, on December 8, Yamasaki's father was fired from the job he had held for thirty years. Shortly thereafter, the government decided to relocate all of the Japanese Americans on the West Coast. Yamasaki decided to bring his parents to New York to live with him in their one-bedroom apartment, rather than let them go to a camp. They lost all their belongings, nevertheless, because they had to leave the west coast so quickly.

From 1943 to 1945, Yamasaki worked for Harrison and Fouilhoix and for Raymond Loewy Associates and taught architectural design at Columbia University. In 1945, the large design firm of Smith, Hinchman & Grylls hired him to be their chief designer and Yamasaki moved to Detroit, Michigan. He remained with this company until 1949, when he entered into the partnership of Leinweber, Yamasaki & Hellmuth, which later became Yamasaki, Leinweber & Associates, and eventually, Minoru Yamasaki and Associates.

Yamasaki's career got off the ground when he and two other colleagues from S. H. & G.,

MINORU YAMASAKI

Leinweber and Hellmuth, formed their own partnership. They were commissioned to do the Lambert-St. Louis Municipal Air Terminal, which was completed in 1956. Their work set the standard for a wave of airport buildings designed by top architects all over the United States. Yamasaki decided that the airport should be a great entrance to the city–the city that had sent Lindbergh across the Atlantic. His plan consisted of three pairs of intersecting barrel vaults. The concrete forms were covered in copper, which made the building stand out, not only from the ground, but also from the air. His design won him the American Institute of Architects' First Honor Award in 1956.

During the construction of the air terminal, Yamasaki had to commute between Detroit and St. Louis. He had many arguments and compromises with the engineers and his client. Due to all the stress, Yamasaki developed severe ulcers, and in December 1953, surgeons had to remove two-thirds of his stomach.

Two months after Yamasaki's ulcer attack, he was discharged from the hospital. He was determined to put his life in order and reduce his stress. He decided that he would take the initiative and split the firm, bringing one of the partners with him. George Hellmuth stayed with the St. Louis firm and eventually became a very large company. Minoru now was head of his own firm and he could accept the commissions that would produce the least stress. He was no sooner back at work than he was requested by the State Department to design a new consulate general in Kobe, Japan. He traveled to Japan and spent hours studying the ancient temples in their garden settings. "It was here that I decided that serenity could be an important contribution to our environment because our cities are so chaotic and full of turmoil," he said.

Yamasaki did his best to achieve "the joy of surprise" as he called it.

After his trip to Japan and other parts of the world, Yamasaki turned his efforts away from designing really big projects, and focused on smaller ones. Yamasaki did his best to achieve "the joy of surprise" as he called it. In August 1955, Detroit's dull Wayne State University hired Yamasaki to design the McGregor Memorial Community Conference Center. He believed that the building should be a gateway between the city and the campus, and he designed an open glass gallery with conference rooms on either side. The McGregor Conference Center's pool of water, environment-controlling wall, and central hall with skylights are all features that are common to many Yamasaki-designed buildings. The building was designed soon after his first trip around the world and he tried to express some of the architectural influences he had encountered. When the Conference Center opened in 1958, there was a ceremony, in which

Yamasaki was asked to give a speech. When he finished, he was stunned to find that every person in the place was on his feet clapping. They were so happy to have such a beautiful building. Architectural magazines called McGregor Center "delightful" and "refreshing." He received another First Honor Award from the American Institute of Architects for this building in 1959.

He went on to design the Reynolds Metal Company Building on the outskirts of Detroit, which has been described by its owners as a "jewel on stilts." His clients asked him to design a building that would focus attention on aluminum since the automotive industry was located primarily in Detroit. His design won him a third First Honor Award. Among his other accomplishments are the Science Pavilion for the Seattle 1962 World's Fair, the Michigan Consolidated Gas Company Building that rises thirty stories on one side of Detroit's Civic Center, a gracefully vaulted synagogue in Glencoe, Illinois, and the Woodrow Wilson School of Public and International Affairs at Princeton University.

Yamasaki is perhaps best known for his design of the World Trade Center on the Lower West Side of Manhattan, New York. In 1962, Yamasaki received a letter from Richard Sullivan of the Port Authority of New York and New Jersey, who, along with Malcolm Levy, had been assigned the task of finding the architect for the World Trade Center. The World Trade Center was to house anything and anyone connected with world trade and it was to be very big. Sullivan indicated that the cost would be in the neighborhood of $280,000,000, which Minoru believed to be too big a project for his fifty-five man office to handle. (The final cost of the project far exceeded the initial estimates.) He competed for the job, even though he was sure it would be a waste of time. Minoru Yamasaki and Associates had a wonderful celebration in their office when they learned they had received the commission to do the design.

The twin towers of the World Trade Center have brought great pride to Lower Manhattan.

Yamasaki designed twin 110-story buildings intended to give a soaring feeling. The Trade Center Towers are set back from the Church Street entrance and the plaza offers sculptures, rings of benches, and a 130-foot circle of flower boxes that offer some tranquility in the busy New York workplace.

Even after all this success, "Yama" as his friends used to call him, met with much discrimination outside the world of architecture. When he first became a success and began to accumulate wealth, Yamasaki decided to move his family to a larger house. He asked his real estate agent to find him a house in either Birmingham, Bloomfield Hills, or Grosse Pointe. But he soon found out that even though he was Detroit's most prominent architect, he was still a nisei (second-generation Japanese American), and therefore, an outsider. His real estate broker told him, "I can't get you a house in either suburb, Yama. But I know of a fine old farmhouse in Troy which you can have." Yama liked the house, which was over a century old. He surrounded the house with Japanese-style gardens and patios and put in a deep Japanese-style bath. Yamasaki was never bitter over his treatment as a Japanese American. "Only in America can people like myself get anywhere or try to do the things they want to do," he said.

"Only in America can people like myself get anywhere or try to do the things they want to do."

Minoru and his wife, Teruko, had three children: Carol, born in 1944, Taro, born in 1945, and Kim, born in 1947. Carol Yamasaki is a t'ai chi instructor and is married to Christopher Hayes. The couple have two children, Jesse and Naomi. Taro is a contributing photographer to People Weekly and received a Pulitzer in 1981. He and his wife Susan have three children: Takei, Seth, and Shantih. Kim, who worked in his father's firm from 1979 until his father died, became chief executive officer of the firm from 1987 until 1990. Kim is currently the director of new project development for the country's largest cooperatively managed non-profit senior citizen housing management development company. He and his wife Maria have three children, Moriko, Katie, and Matt. Teruko (Teri) Yamasaki continues to live in the beautiful

From left to right, Kim, Carole, Taro, Teruko, and Minoru Yamasaki.

house that Yama designed and built for her in 1972 in Bloomfield Hills, Michigan, which was, not coincidentally, one of the locations that the Yamasakis were denied a house in the 1940's.

At one time, the offices of Minoru Yamasaki and Associates had eighty employees and grossed millions of dollars. But no matter how hectic his days got, Yama paid attention to every detail of his designs, down to the doorknobs. He also made sure he knew all of his employees by name! Yamasaki tried to treat all of his employees and associates with the respect they deserved as professionals. This was especially important to him since he always remembered the inhumane treatment he received for five summers working in the Alaskan fish canneries. But this did not mean he would accept less than one-hundred percent effort from all his staff. One day, a client was scheduled to visit the office to interview them for a design job. Like usual, the office was cluttered with old, unnecessary drawings and papers. The building maintenance was not good, so the floors were dirty and unswept. Yamasaki decided that all the office employees had to help clean up, and Yama was sweeping the floors himself. All at once he noticed that while everyone else was working, a young man that was recently hired was just sitting on a stool in the corner. Yamasaki asked him why he wasn't helping. "I was hired to be an architect, not a janitor," was the young man's reply. Yamasaki promptly fired him on the spot!

Minoru Yamasaki and Associates still exists today, but as a much smaller company than it once was. Minoru Yamasaki died on February 6, 1986, in Detroit, Michigan. He was 73 years old and has been credited with the design of more than three hundred buildings. Though in his own words, Yamasaki admitted to "designing some real dogs," all of his work was carried out with love and dedication. His buildings are a permanent memorial to his life.

KRISTI YAMAGUCHI

Figure Skater
1971-

"I am so surprised that everything in my skating career happened so fast. I've trained for and dreamed about the Olympics since I was a little girl and first put on a pair of skates. Dreams do come true."

Kristi Yamaguchi, July 1993

AS YOU READ

- As you read, see if you can determine what has motivated Kristi to be the best skater she can be.
- When you read the story, you will find that Kristi's family does not like to discuss their ordeal during World War II. Can you speculate why?
- Kristi's family has been in America for nearly a century. Do you think this makes her immune to ethnic prejudice?
- Two other skaters at the 1992 Winter Olympics were able to perform the very difficult triple axel jump. But Kristi did not feel she was at a disadvantage because she had not perfected this jump for her program. Why did it turn out she was right?

Kristi Yamaguchi

Skating into our hearts and into the homes of millions of American television viewers, Kristi Yamaguchi performed in the 1992 Winter Games in Albertville, France on February 19 as if all that mattered was giving us enjoyment. Skating to Strauss's *Blue Danube Waltz*, she floated from one required element of her program to the next and won the highest scores from all nine judges. While all the other world's top female skaters cracked under the pressure to outjump the others, Kristi performed all of her jumps with ease. Two days later during the free skate, she again committed far fewer errors than her competitors, thus capturing the gold medal for the United States. In 1992, at the age of twenty, little five-foot, ninety-two pound Kristi Yamaguchi became the first American woman to win the Olympic championship title in figure skating since Dorothy Hamill in 1976.

Kristi Yamaguchi always dreamed of learning to skate well enough to compete in the Winter Games. She began taking skating lessons at the age of six and quickly demonstrated a natural talent for the sport. Born on July 12, 1971, in Hayward, California, Kristi Tsuya Yamaguchi was one of three children born to Jim Yamaguchi and Carole (Doi) Yamaguchi. Her father is a dentist and her mother is a medical secretary. She grew up in Fremont, which like Hayward, is in the San Francisco Bay area. She graduated from Mission San Jose High School. Both of her siblings are also sports enthusiasts. Her older sister, Lori, was on a championship baton-twirling team, and her brother, Brett, plays high school basketball.

Kristi Yamaguchi always dreamed of learning to skate well enough to compete in the Winter Games.

Both sides of Kristi's family have lived in the United States for almost one-hundred years. They have been here long before Congress wrote the Immigration Act of 1924, designed to keep the Japanese out. Regardless of the long duration that the families have been here, her parents and grandparents endured considerable hardship during World War II, when they, along with 110,000 other Japanese Americans were required by the United States government to be relocated to internment camps. Carole Doi's father (Kristi's maternal grandfather) was attending the University of Southern California, and with the rest of his family, was sent off to a camp in Colorado. Soon after, he enlisted in the U. S. Army and was sent off to Germany to fight with the other U. S. Troops. Kristi's mother, Carole, was born in camp. Kristi's grandmother's family lost all of their possessions including their nursery in Gardenia.

The Yamaguchi's similarly lost their ranch and all that belonged to them. But, despite their hardship, they have only rarely discussed this time in their lives with Kristi and her brother and sister. They have encouraged their children to appreciate American values and to work hard. "My grandfather didn't talk much about World War II, but he let me know how proud he was to see me make it as an Asian American representing the United States. My parents let us know how fortunate we are now. Otherwise, they really don't look back on it too much." Mrs. Yamaguchi is reluctant to talk about any of this because, it seems, it was a long time ago and none of them wishes to dwell on it anymore.

In 1976, Kristi saw Dorothy Hamill win the women's Olympic singles title. From then on, Kristi wanted to be a figure skater. When she was eight years old, she took part in her first competition. In the following year, she started a rigorous training schedule. She arose at four o'clock each morning to practice at the local ice skating rink before going to school.

Kristi has also skated and competed in pairs, which meant that she only practiced singles half the time. In 1983, Kristi and Rudi Galindo started to pair skate. Rudi needed to find someone small, like himself (he was four-foot, six inches at the time) to skate with. Under Jim Hulick, their pairs coach, they scored their first success in 1985 when they finished fifth in the National Junior Championships. Kristi also placed fourth in the Novice National Competition in singles. By the next year, Kristi and Rudi had taken first place. Kristi also emerged as a challenger in singles tournaments as well. In 1986, she became the Central Pacific junior champion and qualified again to compete in the national junior medal event. She finished fourth in this competition.

In 1988, she was a gold medalist in both the singles and the pairs categories at the World Junior Championships held in Brisbane, Australia. That year, the Women's Sports Foundation named her the Up-and-Coming Artistic Athlete of the Year.

Kristi at eight years old

In 1989, Kristi won her first senior title, a gold medal in the pairs competition at the National Championships in Baltimore, Maryland. She also placed second in the singles division and became the first woman to win two medals at the National Championships since Margaret Graham did so thirty-five years before.

After her strong performance at the nationals, Kristi competed for the first time in the 1989

World Championships held in March in Paris, France. She finished as the sixth-best singles skater in the world, and she and Galindo finished as the fifth-best pairs skaters.

In the next three years before the Winter Games, Kristi's life turned upside down. First, her long-time coach, Christy Kjarsgaard married Andrew Ness, a Canadian physician in the spring of 1989 and moved to Edmonton, Alberta. Kristi decided to follow her coach to Canada and left California the day after she graduated from high school. She lived with the Nesses for two years and then finally moved out on her own. Her pairs partner, Rudi Galindo, also went to Canada, and this meant that both of them had to divide their time between Edmonton and San Francisco to continue their pairs training with Jim Hulick. The arrangement worked okay for a while, but then Jim Hulick died in December 1989 of colon cancer. At about the same time, Kristi's maternal grandfather also died. "They were two big influences on me as a skater," she is quoted as saying. "They used to be the happiest seeing me go on. They made me work harder."

It became more and more difficult for Kristi to divide her time traveling between San Francisco and Edmonton for singles and pairs training, and so in May 1990, Kristi decided to withdraw from pairs competition and devote her time exclusively to singles competition.

Kristi with her family. From left to right, Carole, Kristi, Brett, Lori, and Jim Yamaguchi.

After the major competitions were concluded in July 1990, the compulsory figures were eliminated from future competition. This was good news for Kristi since this wasn't a strong area for her. Now that she no longer had to practice pairs or her compulsories, Kristi was free to concentrate on her preparation for the singles competition. In the second half of 1990, she quickly showed herself to be one of the top three female singles skaters in the world.

Kristi has lost competitions to Midori Ito of Japan, the only woman in the world to have successfully landed the notoriously difficult triple axel by 1990. In February 1991, Tonya Harding became the second female to land the triple axel in competition. The Royal Glenora Club, where Kristi was training daily, installed a special jumping harness to help her and other skaters master the jump, named for its inventor, Axel Paulsen. But she had not perfected it before the Winter Games.

In the 1991 world competition, Kristi easily took the world crown. She skated a nearly perfect short program and gave one of the best free-skate performances of her career. And so, going into the 1992 Winter Olympics as the reigning United States and world figure skating champion, Kristi became the focus of intense media speculation. It was written that Midori Ito and Tonya Harding had the edge because they could land the triple axel. The media put tremendous pressure on all the skaters. But, Kristi had not planned any triple axels in her program. Instead, she had seven other triples planned, including a triple-lutz and a triple-toe combination, which she felt made hers one of the most difficult programs. She did not feel she needed a triple axel to take the gold. As it turned out, she was right. As each of Kristi's female rivals tumbled to the ice during their program, Kristi made it look so easy.

In the following month, Kristi went on to win her second world championship, becoming the first American female skater to defend her world title since Peggy Fleming did so in 1968.

Kristi won the Gold Medal in Figure Skating at the 1992 Winter Olympics in Albertville, France.

After the Olympic Games, Kristi hired an agent, Kevin Albrecht to negotiate endorsements for her. An article in *Business Week* speculated that Kristi would not receive a lot of endorsements because of her Japanese surname and Japanese looks. But, Kristi did go on to get some good endorsements. She has an agreement with Kellogg's Special K cereal and with the Hoechst Celanese Corporation, which manufactures acetate fibers. She also has contracts with Durasoft Contac lenses, California Raisin Board, and the Bank of Hawaii.

Kristi has worked extensively with the "Make-a-Wish" Foundation and is in her second year as the Christmas Seal spokesperson for the American Lung Association.

Right now, Kristi is very happy competing as a professional skater. She is one of the headline skaters for the professional tour of "Stars on Ice." At her young age, Kristi has accomplished much to be proud of. Her hard work and determination have proven to us all that dreams really can come true.

For the past two years, Kristi has been the Christmas Seal Spokesperson for the American Lung Association.

AN WANG

Entrepreneur, Founder of Wang Laboratories
1920-1990

"I am never quite able to convince people that I did not suffer culture shock when I arrived in the United States. People insist that I must have been overwhelmed by the things that make America different from China--the wealth, the people, even the food. But this is simply not true. I look for the similarities between cultures, not the differences."

An Wang, *Lessons* (Addison-Wesley)

AS YOU READ

- Keep in mind that An Wang was born in China, though he spent most of his life in the United States. He was also in China during World War II, and this event affected him differently from other Asian Americans who were in the U.S. at the time. Read to find out exactly how World War II affected the direction of Wang's life.

- Wang met his wife, Lorraine Chiu here in the United States. Though both of them were from Shanghai, China, they had not met there. What does this tell you about the migration of the Asians in America?

- Read to find out some of the reasons that Dr. Wang decided to go into business for himself. What did he have to prove?

An Wang

On June 30, 1951, with his entire life savings of about $600, An Wang rented two hundred square feet of office space at about $70 a month in a loft above an electrical fixtures store on Columbus Avenue at the South End of Boston. On his first day of business, he had no orders, no contracts, and no office furniture. He was Wang Laboratory's only full-time employee. By 1986, the company had over thirty thousand employees working in several buildings in Lowell, Massachusetts, and in factories and offices throughout the world.

In 1956, Wang's yearly business income was a modest $10,000. In March of that year, IBM finally settled a patent dispute with him, for which he was paid about $400,000. An Wang became a wealthy man almost overnight. In 1981, Wang Laboratories earned about $100 million on revenues of nearly $1 billion. By the mid-1980's An Wang had a net worth of $1.6 billion, which made him the fifth-richest man in the United States. Despite his wealth and good fortune, Wang lived a quiet, family-oriented life...and never owned more than two suits at any one time!

Born in Shanghai, China on February 7, 1920, to middle class Chinese parents named Yin Lu Wang and Zen Wan (Chien) Wang, An Wang was the oldest son of five children. His name means "Peaceful King."

Wang's father was well educated for his time. He had spent a year at Chiao Tung University (later called Jiao Tong University) at a time when very few Chinese went to college at all. He taught English in a private elementary school in Kun San, about thirty miles from where the Wang family lived in Shanghai. His mother was a loving, caring person, and not at all strict.

Wang lived a quiet, family-oriented life...and never owned more than two suits at any one time!

Until he was twenty-one, he lived in either Shanghai or Kun San, where his father's family had lived for six hundred years. His older sister, Hsu, died in 1945, during the Japanese invasion of China in World War II. He had a younger sister named Yu, and two brothers, Ping and Ge. Because he went away to school at age thirteen, he was not close to his younger brothers and sisters. His schooling, then the war, and finally his travels to the United States kept him separated from his brothers and sisters for forty years.

In 1926, Wang was old enough to go to school; but, the private school that his father taught at had no kindergarten, first, or second grade. So his father enrolled him in the third grade at the age of six. He was always two years younger than his classmates, and much smaller.

AN WANG

> Wang graduated high school at the age of sixteen and entered Chiao Tung University. At that time, Chiao Tung was perhaps the most prestigious university in China.

The Chinese place a much higher value on elementary education than we do in America. This is probably because fewer children actually go to school in China than in the United States. In China, during the early 1930's, children had to take a competitive exam in order to go to a public junior high. Even if you were accepted, your family had to pay for your education. School was not free as it is here in the United States. When Wang finished sixth grade, his parents asked him to wait a year before trying to go to junior high. His grades had not been good in elementary school and his parents felt he might profit if he were a little older. But Wang wanted to continue his education, and he took the exams anyway. He scored the highest of any of the applicants!

In junior high, Wang continued to do poorly in many of his subjects. He only liked the sciences: physics and math. He also liked to read. By age thirteen, he was ready to take the exam to go to high school. He entered Shanghai Provincial High School, which had one of the best academic reputations in all of China. But, Wang had to board at the school and live apart from his family.

He graduated high school at the age of sixteen and entered Chiao Tung University (where his father had gone) in Shanghai. At that time, Chiao Tung was perhaps the most prestigious university in China. Wang was made class president because he had the highest college entrance exam scores of his class. For four years, he studied electrical engineering with an emphasis on communications.

During his four years at the University, World War II was in progress, the Japanese invaded China, and war was all around. Both of his parents and his older sister died during this time. Somehow, Wang managed to finish his college education.

Wang graduated from Chiao Tung in 1940. In the summer of 1940, Wang felt it was necessary to help the war effort. He signed on to design and help build transmitters and radios for the government troops for the Central Radio Corporation. He left Shanghai to travel to central China, which was lucky since just a few months later, Japan attacked Pearl Harbor in the United States and Shanghai became unsafe for both Chinese and foreigners.

During the war, Wang had heard about a program to send some Chinese engineers to the United States on an apprentice program so that they could learn skills to return to China and help China rebuild after the war. Wang was accepted into this program and came to the United States in 1945 to serve a two-year apprentice as a technical observer in American industry.

However, when Wang got to the United States, he decided he would like to get an advanced degree from Harvard instead, and because the war was not officially over (Japan did not surrender until late summer that year), Wang found that Harvard had lots of openings. He still intended to return to China in two years. Instead, Wang ended up staying in the United States; he received a doctorate degree from Harvard, and he founded Wang Laboratories six years later.

From 1948 to 1951, Wang worked in the Harvard Computation Laboratory under Howard Aiken. Aiken and his colleagues had designed the first binary computer (see glossary) in the United States to be operated by electricity. Aiken asked Wang to find a way to record and read magnetically stored information without mechanical motion within the computer. It took Wang about three weeks to come up with the answer. His magnetic pulse device helped develop magnetic memory cores, which became the basis for computers for the next twenty years. He later patented his invention and went on to found Wang Laboratories.

In 1948, Wang met his wife, Lorraine Chiu. They married in 1949 and settled down in the Boston area to raise their family. Lorraine was also from Shanghai, China, though Wang had never met her before he came to the United States. Their first son, Frederick, was born in

September 1950. During the next twelve years, they had two more children, another son, Courtney, and a daughter, Juliette.

In the early 1950's, computers began to be available commercially and Harvard did not want to continue research in this field. They felt that private companies should now continue this research. Wang decided that he no longer wanted to stay at Harvard because of their de-emphasis on computer research and he and Lorraine decided that he should make a go of it on his own. Many of their Chinese friends thought that they were making a mistake. They felt that there was still discrimination in the United States against the Chinese and that Wang could not succeed in industry. Most Chinese Americans stayed in academia or owned restaurants and Chinese laundries. Wang wanted to prove that Chinese Americans could excel in other areas, too.

Wang wanted to prove that Chinese Americans could excel in other areas, too.

Within three weeks of opening his business, Wang received his first orders. He was selling his magnetic memory cores for $4 each. Mostly his early business was in consulting and designing custom, proprietary devices. His next success from engineering was his custom digital devices like the first digitally programmed scoreboard that he designed for Shea Stadium in New York. He developed a phototypesetting machine, the Linasec, under contract to Compugraphic Corporation, which was marketed by Compugraphic in 1963. He went on to develop desktop calculators and in 1976, introduced his revolutionary wordprocessing system that became the standard in wordprocessing for the next ten years.

"I used to get a lot of ideas [about my business] while driving home from work," writes Wang in his book, *Lessons* (Addison-Wesley). "This is one reason that my associates finally prevailed on me to accept a chauffeur. They were afraid that I would get so caught up in thinking about a problem that I might not pay attention to an oncoming truck, and they felt it would be better for both me and Wang Laboratories if I did not drive while thinking about work. In general, I do not have much interest in the ostentation that is commonly associated with being the CEO of a large corporation..... I prefer to have lunch by myself, and I generally use the time to read and think."

Wang always seemed to have the foresight to develop what the American public wanted...But somehow, Wang failed to recognize the microcomputer age until it was upon him.

Wang always seemed to have the foresight to develop what the American public wanted. He liked to manufacture solutions to problems. He felt he should "find a need and fill it." This is what Wang Laboratories did for many years. But Wang somehow failed to recognize the microcomputer age until it was upon him. His peak years at Wang Laboratories coincided with the introduction of microcomputers, and he did not see this until 1983. He tried quickly to supply the market with products the public seemed to want and ended up announcing the introduction of products that did not exist - and that he could not manufacture in time. In 1986, he turned over control of the company to his son, Frederick, but the company continued to decline in the latter 80's as personal computers manufactured by IBM and Apple MacIntosh invaded the market. Wang struck a deal with IBM to resell IBM PC's, but was never able to successfully compete in the personal computer arena.

Wang (left) received a plaque honoring him as an inductee to the National Hall of Fame in 1988. The honor was presented by Sidney William Jr.

Dr. An Wang died in 1990 from cancer of the esophagus. Control of Wang Laboratories is no longer with the Wang family, who owns only thirty-seven percent of the company as of 1993. The present owners filed for bankruptcy in August 1992, more than forty years after the founding of Wang Laboratories.

CONNIE CHUNG

Broadcast Journalist
1946-

"I have no illusions about becoming a weekday anchor," said Connie Chung in a 1983 interview. "My dreams are much more realistic-like landing on Jupiter!"

Connie Chung, *People Weekly,* June 13, 1983

AS YOU READ

- Connie Chung reports the news, but she always seems to be making news of her own. Read to see what recent changes have been made at CBS that include her.
- In the story, Connie tells us what contributed to her luck at being hired by CBS. Read to find out why. Why is Connie's story of discrimination different than what we read about in An Wang's life?
- Some people are insensitive about Connie's success. They insinuate that she has been promoted for other reasons than she is good at what she does. Read to find out how Connie Chung handles these insensitive remarks.
- In Connie's quote above, she indicates in 1983 that it would be difficult for her to obtain a position as a weekday anchor. It was not until 1993 that she became a weekday co-anchor with Dan Rather for CBS News. What does this tell you about women in broadcast journalism?

Connie Chung

It's not like the dark-eyed, black-haired Connie Chung ever thought she could attain the fame in broadcast journalism that she has today. She has always been very realistic about her goals and ambitions. Though she has been often called a workaholic, she does not pretend to be the 90's-type woman who can do it all. She says she is not the type who can work, run a household, do charity work, sew, iron, and make pasta with every hair in place. "I think that's nauseating," she has been quoted as saying.

She confesses that she did try to cook once. She wanted to make a stew for her mother's birthday. After she let the ingredients simmer for twelve hours, the meal was nearly inedible. "My mother looked at me with total understanding," says Connie, "and said, 'It's all right, dear. You were meant to do the news.' "

According to many in the news industry, Connie Chung, along with ABC's Barbara Walters and CBS's Diane Sawyer, is one of the three most successful, visible, powerful, and influential of all network newswomen. For over twenty-two years she has been reporting the news. She has won three emmy awards. Her light-hearted humor has contributed to her success and popularity. She once referred to herself as "America's best known 'yellow journalist!'"

Connie Chung

Born on August 20, 1946, in Washington, D.C., Constance Yu-hwa Chung was the tenth and youngest child of William Ling Chung and Margaret (Ma) Chung. Five of her siblings died in China during World War II. William Ling Chung, an intelligence officer in Chiang Kai-shek's government in China, decided to move his wife and four surviving daughters from Shanghai, China to Washington D.C., just at the height of the Japanese bombing of China in 1944. When Mao Zedong and the Communist Party won the Chinese Revolution in 1949, Chung decided not to return his family to China. Connie was the only member of the family to be born in the United States.

Connie grew up in the Maryland suburbs of Washington, D.C. She was active in school politics. Her classmates included such well-known personalities as actress Goldie Hawn and Watergate journalist, Carl Bernstein.

As the youngest girl, Connie felt somewhat intimidated by her older sisters. She was not very outgoing while she was growing up, so her sisters were shocked when she decided to become a news reporter. Connie did appear in high school plays and variety shows and she took an active part in her student government. Connie remembers a childhood of parties and

Connie Chung, along with ABC's Barbara Walters and CBS's Diane Sawyer, is one of the three most successful, visible, powerful, and influential of all network newswomen.

picnics. "We were a big, wonderful family," says Chung.

"They had one woman at CBS at the time, and I think they wanted to hire more."

In 1965, Connie entered the University of Maryland as a biology major. Between her junior and senior years, she worked as a summer intern to Seymour Halpern, a Republican congressman from New York. She wrote speeches and press releases for him. She enjoyed this so much, she switched her major to journalism when she returned to college in September. She then went to work part-time as a copy clerk with WTTG, a television station in the capital. When she graduated in 1969, she became a news department secretary at WTTG and soon was promoted to a newswriter.

Connie actually met her husband, Maury Povich, for the first time in 1969 when he was the very popular host of the talk show *Panorama* in Washington D.C. Though she remembers Maury the first time they met, he was married at the time, and he doesn't remember that meeting with Connie very well. Connie says, "I find this *soooo* insulting!"

Connie went on to become an assignment editor and later, an on-air reporter at WTTG.

In 1971, the Federal Communications Commission was pressuring the television networks to hire more minorities and women. Connie applied for a job at CBS's Washington Bureau. "They only had one woman at CBS at the time, and I think they wanted to hire more. So they hired me, they hired Leslie Stahl, they hired Michelle Clark (a black reporter who died in a plane crash the following year), and they hired Sylvia Chase. In other words, a Chinese woman, a black woman, a nice jewish girl, and a blonde shiksa [a jewish term for a gentile woman]. Perfect. And so they took care of years of discrimination [all at once]."

"I would definitely say that being Asian and a woman helped me get hired. [At the time], it was a male-dominated profession." Over the years, she has had many insensitive questions about her rise at CBS. Years ago, when a CBS News executive asked her how a young female, Chinese American reporter had advanced so far, Connie pointed to Bill Small (who was the news division's senior Vice President at the time) and proclaimed, "Bill likes the way I do his shirts!"

"I would definitely say that being Asian and a woman helped me get hired..."

Connie was made a general assignment political reporter at CBS. She was willing to tackle any assignment. She covered the Watergate hearings in the early 1970's and was always following key figures in the scandal, such as John Dean, John Mitchell, John Ehrlichman, and Bob Haldeman.

CONNIE CHUNG

In 1976, Connie Chung became a news anchor on KNXT (now KCBS), the local CBS television station in Los Angeles, California. She did news telecasts three times a day. She took the station from third place in the ratings to second, and by 1983, she was reportedly the highest-paid local news anchor in the country.

Connie with husband, Maury Povich at a New York Knicks game at Madison Square Garden, June 1993

She stayed in Los Angeles for seven years, but eventually, she missed the national scene. In 1983, she accepted an offer from NBC to anchor NBC *News at Sunrise*, to serve as a political correspondent for the *NBC Nightly News* program, and to anchor the network's Saturday evening news. Connie was anxious to return to reporting national politics, especially as the 1984 presidential campaigns approached. She reportedly took a large cut in pay to return to New York for NBC. There was also much speculation at that time, that she took the move to be closer to her "sometime" boyfriend, Maury Povich, who lived on the east coast. As Connie said at the time, "Had I been male, people would have merely thought it was a career move." But then she went on, "We hadn't planned to get married, but maybe we were thinking we would give it a chance if we were at least on the same coast."

Povich jokes that Connie had lived alone for so long in her New York apartment that the doorman called him Mr. Chung!

And they did give it a chance! In 1984, Connie and Maury were married. (Maury's first marriage fell apart sometime in the mid 1970's.) They were married in a jewish ceremony in her New York apartment. They had started dating in 1978, but neither one of them was willing to arrange their professional careers to fit their private lives. They carried on a "commuter courtship" for seven years as their work took them to different cities in the United States. At one point, Connie was in Los Angeles and Maury was in Philadelphia. And though they were married in 1984, it was not until 1986 that they were able to move in together! During this time, they rarely saw each other more than once a week. Connie would anchor NBC's Saturday night news, fly to Washington to see Maury, and fly back Sunday late afternoon to get up at 3 am to do NBC's *News at Sunrise.* Finally, Maury got an offer to co-host *A Current Affair* for Fox TV back in New York and the couple could finally be together. Povich jokes that Connie had lived alone for so long in her New York apartment that the doorman called him Mr. Chung!

In 1985, NBC was trying desperately to create a successful prime-time news magazine. Thirteen previous attempts had failed. Connie Chung was named chief correspondent for *American Almanac*, which started out as a monthly series and was supposed to be granted a weekly spot. The program debuted on August 6, anchored by Roger Mudd, but NBC decided to cancel the show in February 1986. Later that year, the show was revamped with Roger Mudd and Connie Chung as co-anchors. Again the show failed to attract viewers and was cancelled that December.

From 1987 to 1989, Connie filed stories for the *NBC Nightly News* and co-wrote and hosted several prime-time documentaries. In the fall of 1987, she visited China for the first time when an NBC news team traveled to Beijing and other cities. She interviewed several of her relatives, including two of her father's first cousins. Her relatives told the history of modern China to the NBC news cameras-how the war had affected the family, how the cultural revolution had affected them. Because it was Connie's family that she was interviewing, people in the United States watched intently.

In 1987, she hosted the documentary *Scared Sexless*, about how fear of getting AIDS has affected the sexual behavior of the nation. It was the highest-rated NBC news special in a ten-year period.

In 1988, Connie went back into the political arena to cover the 1988 presidential elections. She was a floor correspondent during the national nominating conventions. At the Democratic convention in Atlanta in July, she was the first to interview Jesse Jackson. She was also the first newsperson to interview John F. Kennedy, Jr. after he introduced his uncle, Senator Edward Kennedy.

In March 1989, Connie Chung announced that she would rejoin CBS as an anchor to one of their prime-time news magazines, *West 57th*, would be an anchor for the *CBS Sunday Night News*, and would be a substitute anchor for Dan Rather on the *CBS Evening News*. On June 1, 1993, Connie was appointed to co-anchor the

Likability is her secret weapon that boosts her above other newspersons.

network news with Dan Rather, becoming only the second woman ever to co-anchor a nightly network news broadcast. Connie saw her new appointment as a victory for women: "I think we can thank the wives of these men [CBS news honchos] for raising their consciousness." Dan Rather called Connie, "Miss Congeniality" as he hugged and kissed his new on-air partner. According to a Gannett News Service Story (Sunday, May 23, 1993): "Viewers love her; for several years she's had one of the highest Q-ratings, a common industry measure of popularity, of any woman in network news." At the same time, she also hosted a brand new program for CBS, *Eye to Eye With Connie Chung,* which debuted on June 17, 1993. Her original goal for the news magazine was to anchor *Eye to Eye* and report one story per show herself. But when she received her new anchor duties, Connie said, "It's not my desire to spend my life on the magazine."

According to a recent *USA Today* poll, Connie Chung is the newsperson Americans would most like to have over for dinner. Likability is her secret weapon that boosts her above other newspersons. Her office is decorated with a life-size poster of her husband, Maury, who now hosts his own daytime talk show. They live in a large, pre-war apartment that overlooks Central Park. Much of their home life is engaged in business conversation as they compete against one another over who can get ahold of a news-

Dan Rather and Connie Chung announce that she will co-anchor the CBS nightly news.

worthy person first. A typical dinner conversation Maury says is, "Who did you get today?" She then says, "Who did *you* get today?" Her husband jokes, however, that he has to think up all their fun by himself, including planning all their trips. "She has not planned one vacation in our lives," he says. "She's terrible at recess!"

In a recent interview for his book, *The Imperfect Mirror*, Daniel Paisner quotes Connie as saying that the issue of having children is still unresolved for her. "My mother would really like it," she says. "It took me, you know, the longest time just to get m-m-m-m-married. Now for me to try and say b-b-b. It just takes me a long time to decide these big life decisions... My husband thinks that we should, he thinks I'll be much happier than realizing later that I can't." Though she did announce in 1990 that she and Maury were taking "a very aggressive approach to having a baby," the couple is still childless.

Beautiful clothes are her weakness, but as for other hobbies, Connie says, "All I'm really good at is working."

Connie Chung

Connie Chung is
home again at CBS

CARLOS BULOSAN

Writer
1914(?)-1956

"If you want to know what we are, look upon the farms or upon the hard pavements of the city. You usually see us working, or waiting for work, and you think you know us, but our outward guise is more deceptive than our history."

Carlos Bulosan, "Freedom From Want," *Saturday Evening Post*, 1943

AS YOU READ

- The above quote describes how Carlos Bulosan feels about the plight of the Filipino worker in America in the 1930's and 1940's. Read the story to see how he became involved in changing American attitudes.
- Carlos Bulosan came from a poor family in the Philippines. Read to find out how he paid for his passage to the United States.
- Carlos Bulosan was born a peasant, but died the greatest Filipino American writer of all time. How did Carlos learn to read and write English?

CARLOS BULOSAN

Carlos Bulosan arrived in the United States in 1930, in the middle of the Great Depression. He had followed two of his brothers, Aurelio and Dionisio, to Seattle, Washington, after having sold some of the family land to pay the $75 fee for passage from the Philippines to the United States on the Dollar Line.

The radical Filipino American writer and labor organizer is said to have once left a motel room that he had occupied for about a month and left seventeen unpublished stories in a desk drawer. He used to send stories to his friends and relatives, but would forget to keep a copy for himself! Besides his total carelessness about his work, the only other thing for sure that is known about Carlos Bulosan, is that there is little known about the details of his life. Researchers have found at least three different dates given for his birth, several different opinions about how much schooling he had, and there is no final, comprehensive collection of his writings outside of the manuscript holdings at the University of Washington. Of the facts known for sure, Carlos never returned to the Philippines, and he never became a U.S. citizen.

Carlos Bulosan may have been born on November 2, 1911, or on November 24, 1913 or 1914 to Simeon and Autilia (Sampayan) Bulosan.

He was born in the little Philippine village of Binalonan, in the province of Pangasinan. He had four older brothers and two sisters.

Carlos' family was very poor. He lived in Mangusmana with his father until he was seven. They lived in a small grass hut. His father could not read or write, but he knew how to work the small plot of land to support the family. Carlos helped his father cultivate the family farm. In the spring they planted corn and beans and a few rows of tobacco. The crops were harvested toward the rainy season and stored in the granary. Then they planted rice.

Carlos' family was very poor...They lived in a grass hut. His father could not read or write.

The rest of the family lived in a palm leaf house in Binalonan. Carlos went to school on and off until he was thirteen; then he went for a short while to the public high school in Lingayen. He was expected to help his mother sell vegetables and fish sauce in the neighboring towns. Sometimes he worked as a day laborer in the mongo fields. At the age of twelve, he was employed in a bakery shop. When he was fourteen, he worked in an ice factory, while he went to school. Then he quit school forever and went to work in Baguio, the summer capital of the Philippines.

The family had hoped that an older son, Aurelio, might become a full-fledged schoolteacher, and support the family in a better fashion. They had sent Aurelio to school in Lingayen. Though it was a free, public school, it was far away and the students had to pay for their room and board. Mr. Bulosan sold some of his land to pay for Aurelio's education. The family had deprived themselves of any form of leisure and simple luxury so that Aurelio could finish school. Aurelio needed more money and more money, and threatened to quit school, if he did not receive it. So his father borrowed more money against the remaining family land. They were awaiting the day that Aurelio would teach school and they could repay the loan. Aurelio did finish high school and began to teach sixth grade in Binalonan, but soon the Bulosan farm was lost and Aurelio went to work as a busboy in the United States. Soon, Dionisio followed. Carlos came over a little later.

Even though Carlos was born into a peasant family, he grew up in an atmosphere of change and hope for the future.

Even though Carlos Bulosan was born into a peasant family, he grew up in an atmosphere of change and hope for the future. The laborers and field workers had already begun to emigrate to the United States in large numbers. By 1914, twenty thousand Filipinos had gone to work on the sugar plantations of Hawaii, and some two to three thousand had gone to the west coast--to Washington, Oregon, and California. Within the next fifteen years, nearly one hundred thousand workers went to Hawaii and thirty thousand to California. During the 1920's, the newspapers in the Philippines would run article after article about how wonderful life was in the United States and what success and good fortune Filipinos had found there. There were stories of the Filipino peasant who started out as a lettuce picker in California and quickly became a contractor, earning $1 each day for the hundred or more workers he hired. There were stories of how a bellboy in a hotel could get rich on tips alone. But what really started this "immigration fever" was probably the mail from the United States sent back to family members in the Philippines. The mail contained exaggerated stories of success, an occasional money order, and sometimes, the immigrant would return to his homeland looking very prosperous indeed! All of these factors made the Bulosan brothers decide to make it for themselves in America. Carlos Bulosan came to America full of hope. He was sure he could have a better life in the United States than he had known as a peasant in the Philippines.

Carlos landed in Seattle, Washington on July 22, 1930. He went directly to Lompoc, California to join his brother, Dionisio. But instead of finding a wonderland, Carlos found the United States in the midst of the Great Depression. The glamorous jobs he had heard about did not exist. Carlos soon learned some realities about Filipino life in America. He saw the police come to where he and his brother lived. They took away six other Filipinos who had robbed twenty Japanese. He saw a Filipino pool hall operator

living a block away shoot an American with whom he had an argument. Carlos suddenly realized that America was also a land of fears, that America was not really a land of peace.

Carlos also found that his brother, Dionisio, had changed. He was involved in some type of racketeering; and the situation was difficult and frightening for Carlos. Dionisio did find Carlos a job washing dishes in the Lane Cafe, but Carlos was never strong or healthy, and after a few months of working on and off, he went to Los Angeles to stay with his other brother, Aurelio. Aurelio was doing odd jobs in restaurants and he was able to support Carlos, who then spent his time reading in the public library and writing.

To improve working conditions for the Filipinos, Bulosan joined the labor movement, and from 1935 until 1941 attempted to organize migrant workers into unions.

When Carlos came to the United States, he could not read or write English. He educated himself at the Los Angeles Public Library by starting with the children's books. An acquaintance, Alfonso P. Santos, first met Carlos in the library. "In the library I used to see him very often in the departments of literature, sociology, philosophy, and children...In our conversations, he used to tell me about the rising power of the working class. He glorified the working people," Alfonso said.

To improve working conditions for the Filipinos, Bulosan joined the labor movement, and from 1935 until 1941 attempted to organize migrant workers into unions. Though some accounts of his life say he worked the fields, Carlos did not do fieldwork; he was simply not strong enough. He did visit many of the farm areas, however. At the same time, he was writing and publishing. In 1934, he published *The New Tide*, a bimonthly radical literary magazine. He worked on the *Philippine Commonwealth Times* and other newspapers that focused on the problems of Filipino workers.

Carlos was a small, sickly man, and in 1936, he contracted tuberculosis. He spent the next two years in Los Angeles General Hospital. During this time, he could read all he wanted. He read a book each and every day. He had friends who would bring him book after book. It was during this time that he really became a writer. But he received no recognition as a writer until World War II.

As the Depression lifted and the country moved closer to World War II, the status of Filipinos in the United States changed ever so slightly. Now they became the different Asians, the American allies, and were expected to help against the Japanese. About this time, Carlos Bulosan became accepted as a writer in the United States. In 1942, *Letter From America* and *Chorus For America*, two thin volumes of poetry were published. In 1943, *The Voice of Bataan* was published, written in memory of all the fighting men–Filipino, American, Japanese–who died there.

In 1943, the *Saturday Evening Post* published four articles on the four freedoms: Freedom of Speech, Freedom to Worship, Freedom from Want, and Freedom from Fear. Bulosan, who had known hunger for many years, was chosen to write the article Freedom from Want. The opening quote to this story is from this article. Carlos goes on to say:

In 1946, Carlos published his most famous book, *America is in the Heart*.

"...we are not really free unless we use what we produce. So long as the fruit of our labor is denied us, so long will want manifest itself in a world of slaves...When we have enough to eat, then we are healthy enough to enjoy what we eat. Then we have the time and ability to read and think and discuss things. Then we are not merely living but also becoming a creative part of life. It is only then that we become a growing part of democracy..."

The answer is my grand dream of equality among men and freedom for all.

In 1946, Carlos published his most famous work, *America is in the Heart*, which was first published by Harcourt, Brace, and Co., and republished by the University of Washington Press in 1973. Though the work is autobiographical in nature, it is fiction. His friends and family are loosely disguised in this book. Some of the events he describes as happening to himself, in fact happened to others, and not him at all. He wrote this autobiography from the standpoint of all Filipino-Americans. He combined the experiences of many of his fellow countrymen to show the situation the Filipinos faced in America.

Carlos explains why he wanted to write this book so badly. "The answer is my grand dream of equality among men and freedom for all. To give a literate voice to the voiceless one hundred thousand Filipinos in the United States, Hawaii, and Alaska. Above all, and ultimately, to translate the desires and aspirations of the whole Filipino people in the Philippines and abroad in terms relevant to contemporary history.

"Yes, I have taken unto myself this sole responsibility."

When Carlos had worked in Baguio in the Philippines, he had been a houseboy for an American woman named Mary Strandon. Ms. Strandon had been a librarian in Spencer, Iowa, and had saved enough money to travel to the Philippines to paint. When Carlos had his first book published, he traveled back to Iowa, hoping to find her. "But," Carlos said, "...she had been dead for ten years. I wrote her name on a copy of my first book and donated it to the local library. I think that she would have been happy to know that I would someday write a book about her country."

Carlos was weakened by his tuberculosis, but nevertheless, spent the remaining ten years of his life dedicated to labor unions and changing the social attitude toward Filipinos. He became close friends with Josephine Patrick, a Seattle woman who was very involved with the Committee for Protection of the Foreign Born. This organization was concerned about Filipinos who were being threatened with deportation because of their involvement in labor activities. Through his final years of political activity with the Cannery Workers' Union in Seattle and his constant illness, Josephine stood by him.

Despite the difficult times that Bulosan faced in the United States, the racial discrimination, the hunger, and his constant illnesses, he never lost faith. His closing line in *America is in the Heart* reads, "I knew that no man could destroy my faith in America that had sprung from all our hopes and aspirations, ever."

"I knew that no man could destroy my faith in America that had sprung from all our hopes and aspirations, ever."

Carlos Bulosan died in September 1956 in a Seattle hospital just hours after he was admitted. He died from lung congestion, quite obviously related to his bouts with tuberculosis. His obituary lists his age at the time of death as 41, though this depends on when we believe he was born.

On December 11, 1983, the little town of Binalonan, Pangasinan, unveiled a monument and named a street for Carlos Bulosan, the most famous Filipino American writer of all time.

academic *adj.* (ak-a dem-ik) of, or relating to school, or institution of higher learning

ancestor *n.* (an-ses-ter) one from whom a person is descended, such as a grandfather

ancestry *n.* (an-ses-tree) persons who are included in line of descent

applicant *n.* (ap-li-kant) one who applies (for a job or to a school)

apprentice *n.* (a-pren-tes) a person who is learning by practical experience under skilled workers

aspiration *n.* (ahs-per-ay-shun) hopes and dreams

binary computer *n.* (by-na-ree kum-pyou-ter) a computer that operates with a system of numbers having 2 as its base; the digits 0 and 1 are used in binary computers

Caucasian *adj.* (ko-kay-shun) of, or relating to the white race of mankind as indentified by physical features; mostly from Europe; does not include Africans, or persons of southwest Asian descent

celebrity *n.* (se-leb-ri-tee) a person who is celebrated, or honored; as adj., relating to the person who is celebrated

chaos *n.* (kay-os) a state of confusion

colonnade *n.* (kol-i-nayd) column

compulsory *adj.* (kum-pul-se-ree) that which must be done

controversy *n.* (kan-troh-ver-see) a quarrel; differing views; where people do not agree

GLOSSARY

culture *n.* (kul-cher) the beliefs, social forms, habits, and traditions of a racial, religious, or social group of people

culture shock *n.* a sense of confusion and uncertainty that can affect people exposed to a foreign culture, without the proper preparation

custom *n.* (kus-tem) a long-established practice considered as an unwritten law

debut *vb.* (day-byou) a first appearance

discriminate *vb.* (dis-krim-i-nayt) to make a difference in treatment or favor on the basis of other than merit; to treat differently

distinguish *vb.* (dis-ting-wish) to single out; to show a difference

documentary *n.* (dok-you-men-ter-ee) presentation

dominate *vb.* (dom-i-nayt) to overlook from a superior position; to occupy a superior position

emigrate *vb.* (em-i-grayt) to leave one's place of residence or country and live elsewhere

endorsement *n.* (in-door-sment) to express approval publicly; such as endorsing a particular product; to tell the public such product is good

esophagus *n.* (i-saf-i-ges) a muscular tube that goes down the neck

exaggerate *vb.* (ig-zaj-e-rayt) to overstate the truth

foresight *n.* (four-seyt) the ability to see forward

guise *n.* (giz) an external appearance

GLOSSARY

heritage *n.* (her-a-tij) something transmitted or acquired from a predecessor; family legacy; tradition

immigrant *n.* (im-i-grent) a person who comes to a country to take up permanent residence

inedible *adj.* (in-ed-i-bel) not able to be eaten

integral *n.* (in-ti-grel) formed as a unit with another part; essential to completeness

intense *adj.* (in-tents) considerable; to a large degree

intersect *vb.* (in-ter-sekt) to meet and cross at a point

issei *n.* (ee-sayee) first-generation Japanese-American

kimono *n.* (ki-mo-no) a long robe with wide sleeves traditionally worn with a wide sash by the Japanese

migrate *vb.* (my-grayt) to move from one country to another

nisei *n.* (nee-sayee) second-generation Japanese-American; born in the United States to parents of Japanese descent

ostentation *n.* (os-ten-tay-shun) an excessive, showy display

patent *n.* (pat-ent) protected under proprietary rights; making claim for an invention

phototypesetting *adj.* (fo-to-typ-set-ting) setting type in a manner that uses photography; after type is set within machine, page is developed by photographic process

Glossary

prejudice *n.* (prej-i-dis) a preconceived opinion; an adverse opinion that is formed before sufficient knowledge; to judge a person irrationally, based on preconceived notions, rather than on knowledge of the person

prohibit *vb.* (pro-hi-bit) disallow

proprietary *adj.* (pro-pry-i-tar-ee) protected; private; copyrighted

racism *n.* (ray-sizm) a belief that one race is superior to another; belief that race is the primary determining factor in human traits

racketeering *vb.* (ra-ki-teer-ing) obtaining money by doing something illegal

relocate *vb.* (re-lo-kayt) move to another location

reputation *n.* (rep-you-tay-shun) the overall quality or character as judged by people in general

revenue *n.* (re-ve-new) the gross income

scandal *n.* (skan-del) an action that disgraces those associated with it

serenity *n.* (se-ren-i-tee) having the quality of being serene, tranquil, peaceful

siblings *n.* (sib-lingz) brothers and sisters; children born to the same parents

speculation *n.* (spek-you-lay-shun) the act of reflecting or pondering

stereotype *n., adj.* (ste-ree-oh-typ) a standardized mental picture that is held common by members of a group that represents an oversimplified opinion

striptease *n.* (strip-teez) a performance that teases the audience where the dancers take off some of their clothes, piece by piece
submissive *adj.* (sub-miss-iv) quiet and yielding to the authority of others